HAL•LEONARD

pro vocal
BETTER THAN KARAOKE!

ONGBOOK & SOUND-ALIKE CD
VITH UNIQUE *PITCH-CHANGER*™

AMY WINEHOUSE

T0081797

Cover photo Wes Orshoski / Retna Ltd.

ISBN 978-1-4584-1393-2

HAL•LEONARD®
CORPORATION

7777 W. BLUEMOUND RD. P.O. BOX 138' 9 MILWAUKEE, WI 53213

In Australia Contact:
Hal Leonard Australia Pty. Ltd.
4 Lentara Court
Cheltenham, Victoria, 3' 92 Australia
Email: ausadmin@halleonard.com.au

Visit Hal Leonard Online at
www.halleonard.com

AMY WINEHOUSE

Back to Black

Words and Music by Amy Winehouse and Mark Ronson

Just Friends

Words and Music by Amy Winehouse

G7

but that   just ___ hurts. ___

Chorus

Amaj7   B°/A   Amaj7

When _ will we get   the _ time ___ to be ___   just, __ just _

B°/A   Amaj7   B°/A

___ friends? ___   When will _ we get ___   the time to be ___
                                                                                3

Amaj7   B°/A

___   just ___ friends, __ just ___   friends? ___

Interlude

Bm7   E11   Amaj7   Dmaj9   F♯7♭9(♭13)   G7

Chorus

Amaj7   B°/A   Amaj7

When will we get, ___   da, da, da, the time _ to   be _ just ___ friends,   just _

B°/A   Amaj7   B°/A

___ friends? ___   When will we _ get ___   the time to be ___

Amaj7   B°/A   *rit.*   Amaj7

___   just ___ friends, _ just friends? _   Just ___ friends.

Love Is a Losing Game

Words and Music by Amy Winehouse

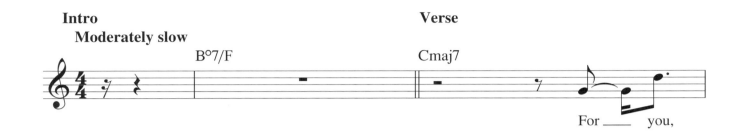

Intro — Moderately slow — B°7/F — Verse — Cmaj7
For ___ you,

G13 — Dm7♭5/F
I was ___ a flame, ___ love is ___ a los -

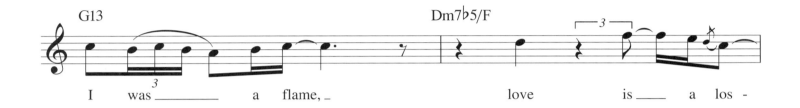

Cmaj7
- ing game. ___ Five ___ sto - ry ___ fi - re as ___

G13 — Dm7♭5/F — Cmaj7
___ you came, ___ love is a los - ing game. ___

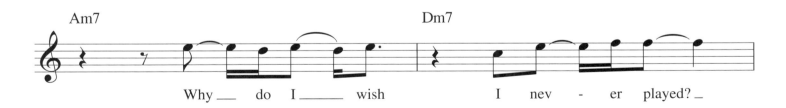

Am7 — Dm7
Why ___ do I ___ wish I nev - er played? ___

Fm7 — Cmaj7
Oh, ___ what a mess we made.

And now the fi - nal ___ frame, _____

love is ___ a los - ing game.

Verse

Played out ___ by _____ the band, ___ love ___ is ___ a los-

- ing hand. _____ More than I _____ could _ stand, _____

love _ is ___ a los - ing hand. _____ Self-pro-fessed,

pro - found, _ 'til the __ chips were ____ down. _____

Know you're _ a gam - blin' man, love is a los-

Verse

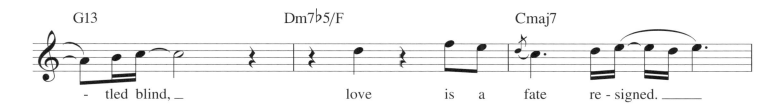

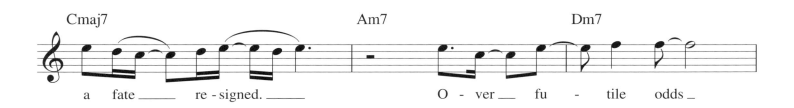

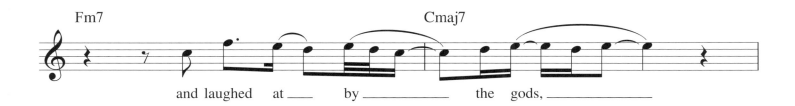

Rehab

Words and Music by Amy Winehouse

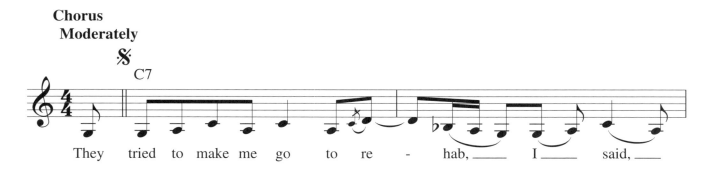

Chorus
Moderately

C7

They tried to make me go to re - hab, I said,

"no, no, no." Yes, I been black, but when

I come back you'll know, know, know.

G7

I ain't got the time, and if my

F7

dad - dy thinks I'm fine, just

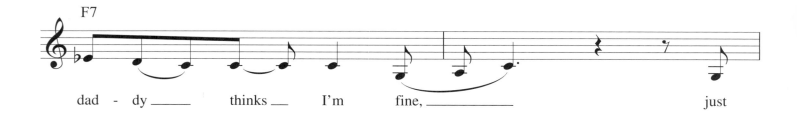

C   F7

try to make me go to re - hab. I won't

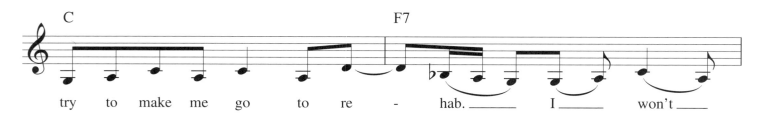

Verse

get a lot in class, _____

F7
but I know _____ it _____ don't come

D.S. al Coda

in _____ a _____ shot glass. They

⊕ Coda
Verse
Em
The man said, "Why do you think you _____

Am   F7
_____ here?"   I said, _____

Ab7
"I got no _____ i - dea. _____

Em
I'm gon - na,   I'm

Am
gon - na lose _____ my _____ ba - by, _____

Verse

I don't ev - er wan - na drink _____

_____ a - gain. I just,

ooh, _____ just _____ need _____ a friend. _____

I'm not _____ gon - na spend _____ ten _____

_____ weeks, _ have ev - 'ry - one

think I'm on _____ the _____ mend. _____

It's not just my pride, _____

It's just _____ 'til these

18

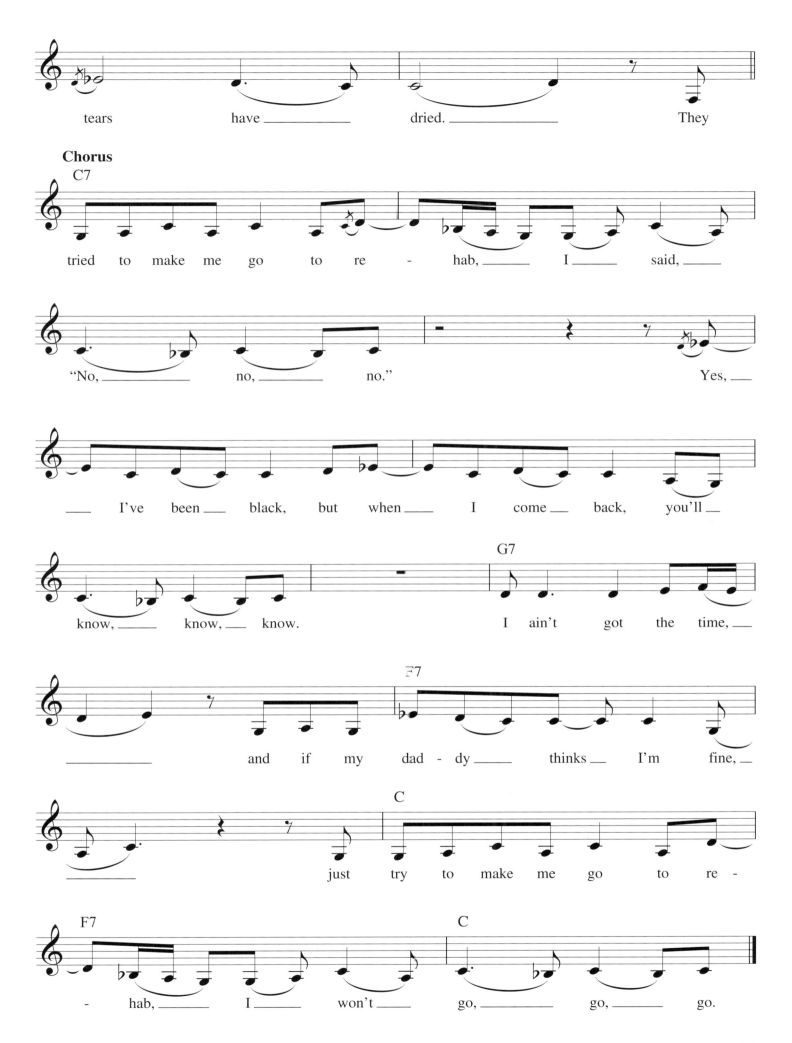

tears   have _____   dried. _____   They

Chorus

C7

tried to make me go to re - hab, _____   I ____ said, ____

"No, _____ no, _____ no."   Yes, ___

___ I've been ___ black, but when ____ I come ___ back, you'll ___

G7

know, _____ know, ___ know.   I ain't got the time, ___

F7

_____ and if my dad - dy _____ thinks ___ I'm fine, ___

C

_____ just try to make me go to re -

F7   C

- hab, _____ I ____ won't ____ go, _____ go, ____ go.

Tears Dry on Their Own

Words and Music by Amy Winehouse, Valerie Simpson and Nickolas Ashford

C#m   A

the sun goes _ down,   he _ takes _ the day, _ but I'm ___ grown. _   And in your _

Esus4/B

___ gray,   in this blue ___ shade, _ my _____ tears dry   on their   own. _

Verse

E/B   F#7/A#

___   I   wish I   could _ say no re - grets   and no e -

A   E/G#   F#m

mo - tion - al ___ debts, _   'cause   as   we   kiss good - bye, ___ the   sun _

A/G#   A7   E/B   F#7/A#

___ sets.   So   we are his - to - ry, _____   your shad - ow cov - ers me, _____

A   E/G#   F#m   G#m

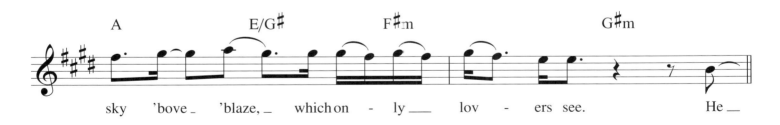

sky 'bove _ 'blaze, _ which on - ly ___ lov - ers see.   He _

Chorus

A   F#m   G#m   C#m   A   F#m   G#m

___ walks _ a - way,   the sun goes _ down,   he _ takes _ the day, _____

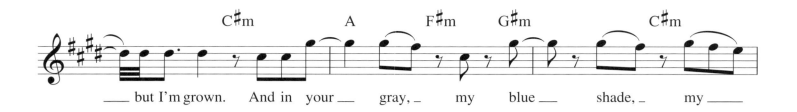

____ but I'm grown. And in your ____ gray, __ my blue __ shade, __ my ____

tears _ dry _ on __ their own. __ Whoa, __ he ____ walks _ a-way,

Chorus

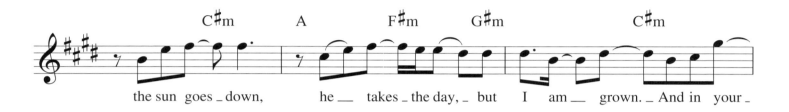

the sun goes _ down, he __ takes _ the day, _ but I am _ grown. _ And in your _

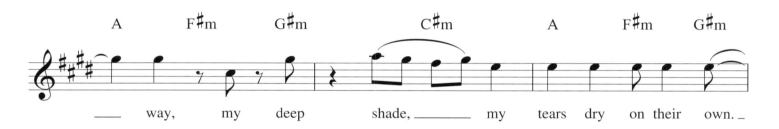

__ way, my deep shade, ____ my tears dry on their own. _

Chorus

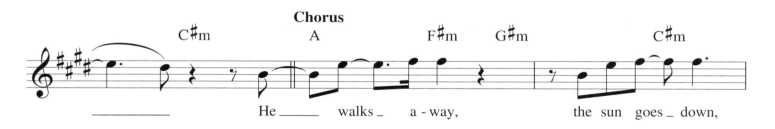

____ He ____ walks _ a-way, the sun goes _ down,

he __ takes _ the day, _ but I'm grown. And in your __ way, my deep

shade, _ my ____ tears dry. ____

Valerie

Words and Music by Sean Payne, David McCabe,
Abigail Harding, Boyan Chowdhury and Russell Pritchard

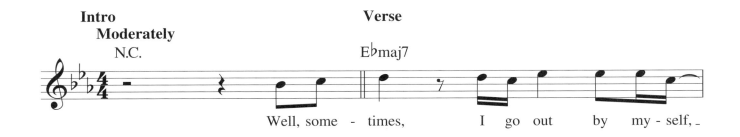

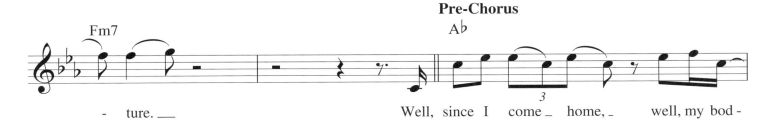

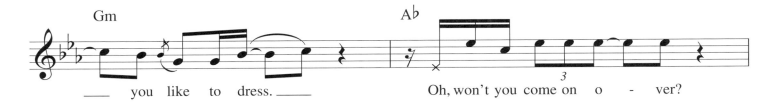

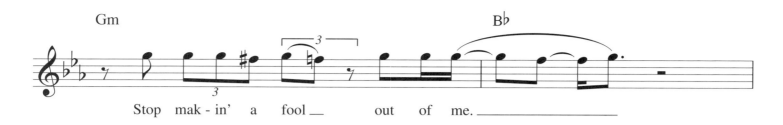

Gm   Bb

Stop mak - in' a fool __ out of me. _____

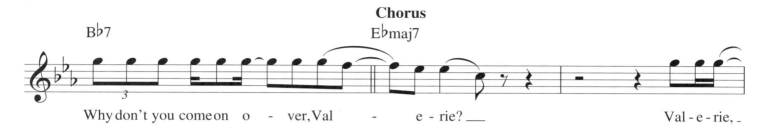

Chorus

Bb7   Ebmaj7

Why don't you come on o - ver, Val - e - rie? __   Val - e - rie, _

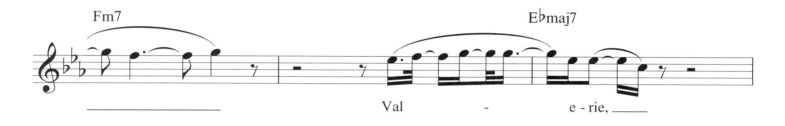

Fm7   Ebmaj7

_____ Val - e - rie, _____

Fm7

Val - e - rie. _____   Did you

Verse

Ebmaj7

have to go to jail, _   put your house on up for sale? _ Did you get a good

Fm7   Ebmaj7

law - yer? _____   I hope you did-n't catch a tan,   I hope

                                      Fm7

you find the right man _ who'll fix it for you. _____   And now, _ you're

Ebmaj7

shop-pin' an - y - where, _ changed the col - or of your hair, _ and are you bus-

Fm7   Ebmaj7

- y?   And did you have to pay _ that fine _ that you were

Fm7

dodg-in' all _ the time? Are you _ still _ diz - zy? _____

Pre-Chorus

Ab   Gm

Since I come a - home, _ well, my bod - y's been a mess, _____ and I miss _

Ab   Gm

_ your ten - der hair _ and the way _ you like to dress. _____

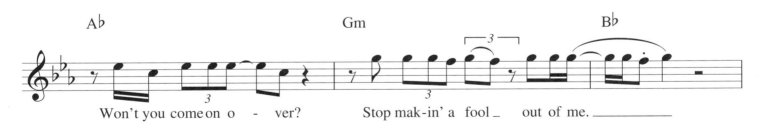

Ab   Gm   Bb

Won't you come on o - ver? Stop mak-in' a fool _ out of me. _____

Chorus

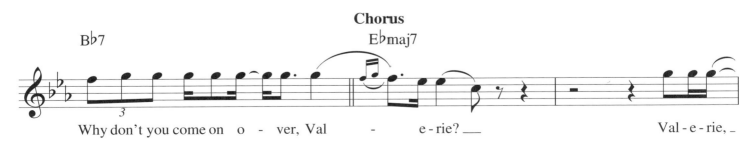

Bb7   Ebmaj7

Why don't you come on o - ver, Val - e-rie? _   Val - e-rie, _

27

Why don't you come on o - ver, Val -

Outro-Chorus

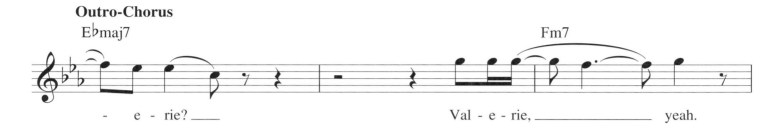

- e - rie? _____ Val - e - rie, _____ yeah.

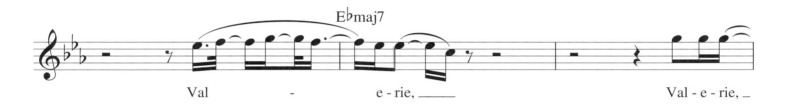

Val - e - rie, _____ Val - e - rie, _

_____ whoa, _____ Val - e - rie, _

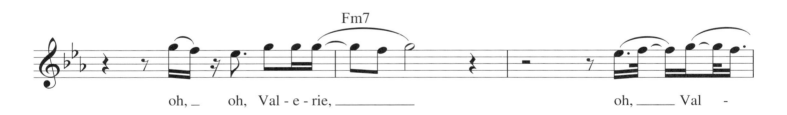

oh, _ oh, Val - e - rie, _____ oh, _____ Val -

- e - rie, _____ Val - e - rie, _____ yeah, _____ Val - e - rie.

Freely

_____ Why don't you come on o - ver, _ Val - e - rie?

Wake Up Alone

Words and Music by Amy Winehouse and Paul O'Duffy

Intro
Slow 2-feel

Verse

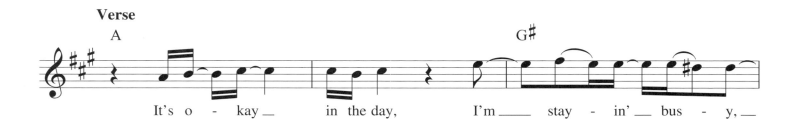

It's o-kay __ in the day, I'm __ stay-in' __ bus-y, __

__ tied up e-nough so I don't have to won-der

where _____ is he. __ Got so sick of cry-

in', so __ just late-ly, __ when I catch __ my-self, __

F#m   F   A

__ I do a ____ one eight - y. ____ I stay up, clean _

G#

__ the house, at least I'm not drink - in'. _____

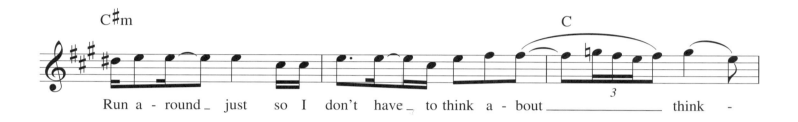

C#m   C

Run a - round _ just so I don't have _ to think a - bout _____ think -

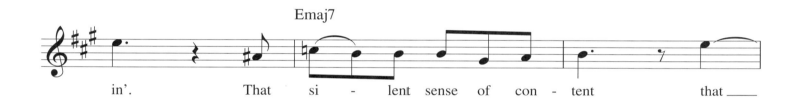

Emaj7

in'. That si - lent sense of con - tent that ____

C#m   C

__ ev-er-y-one _ gets ____ just dis - ap - pears _____ soon

Chorus

F#m   F   D

as the _ sun _ sets. _____ His face in my

G   E

dreams, seiz - ing my guts, _ he _____ floods _ me with dread. ____

Soaked _ in soul, _ he swims in my _____ eyes by _

_ the bed. _____ Pour _ my - self _____ o - ver him, _

moon _____ spill - in' in, _____ and I wake up _____

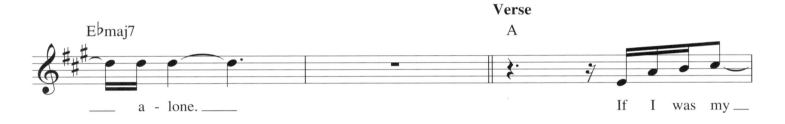

_ a - lone. _____ **Verse** If I was my _

_ heart, _ I'd rath - er be rest - less.

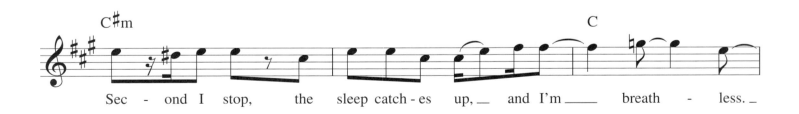

Sec - ond I stop, the sleep catch - es up, _ and I'm _____ breath - less. _

_ 'Cause this ache _ in _ my chest _ as my day is done now, _

C   F#m

the dark cov-ers me, ___ and I ___ can-not ___ run ___ now. _

F   A

My blood ___ run-nin' cold, _____ I ___

G#   C#m

___ stand _ be - fore ___ him. ___   It's

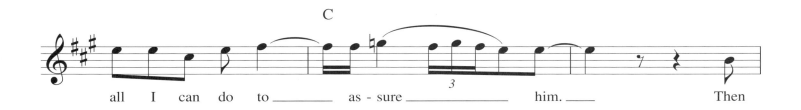

C

all I can do to _____ as - sure _____ him. ___ Then

Emaj7   C#m

he comes ___ to me. ___ I drip _ for ___ him ___ to - night. _

C   F#m

Drown - ing in me, _____ we bathe ___ un - der blue light.

Chorus

F   D

His face in my dreams, _ seiz-ing my guts,

he _____ floods _____ me with dread. _____ Soaked in soul, _____

_____ he swims in ___ my ___ eyes _____ by the bed. _____

Pour my - self o - ver him, moon ___

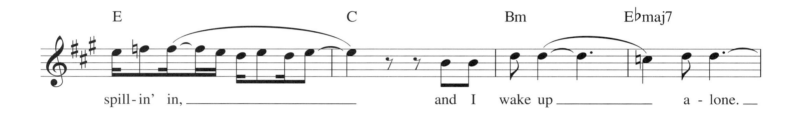

spill-in' in, _____ and I wake up _____ a - lone. ___

Outro

___ And I wake up _____ a - lone, _____

___ and I wake up _____ a - lone, ___

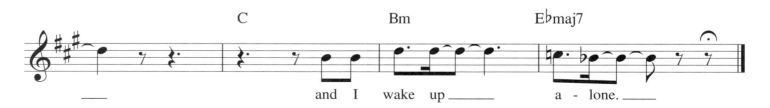

___ and I wake up _____ a - lone. ___

You Know I'm No Good

Words and Music by Amy Winehouse

Intro
Moderately

Verse

Meet you down-stairs _ in the bar _ and hurt, _ your rolled-up _ sleeves _ in your

skull T - shirt. _ You say, "What did you do _ with _ him to-day?" _ and

sniffed me _ out _ like I was Tan-quer - ay. _ 'Cause you're my

Pre-Chorus

fel - la, my guy, _ hand me your Stel - la and fly. _

By the time _ I'm out the door, _ you're ten _ men _ down _ like

cried ___ for ___ you ___ on the kitch - en floor. _____

Chorus

I cheat-ed my - self, ___ like I knew ___ I ___ would. ___

___ I told ya I _____ was trou - ble, ___ you

Interlude

know ___ that I'm no ___ good. ___

Verse

Sweet re - un - ion, Ja - mai - ca ___ and ___ Spain, ___

we're like ___ how ___ we ___ were a - gain. ___ I'm in the tub, ___ you

on the ___ seat, ___ lick your ___ lips ___ as I _____ soak my feet. ___

Pre-Chorus

Then you no - tice lit - tle car - pet burn, ___ my stom - ach drop and ___

Pro Vocal® Series
SONGBOOK & SOUND-ALIKE CD
SING 8 GREAT SONGS
WITH A PROFESSIONAL BAND

Whether you're a karaoke singer or an auditioning professional, the Pro Vocal® series is for you! Unlike most karaoke packs, each book in the Pro Vocal Series contains the lyrics, melody, and chord symbols for eight hit songs. The CD contains demos for listening, and separate backing tracks so you can sing along. The CD is playable on any CD player, but it is also enhanced so PC and Mac computer users can adjust the recording to any pitch without changing the tempo! Perfect for home rehearsal, parties, auditions, corporate events, and gigs without a backup band.

WOMEN'S EDITIONS

00740247	**1. Broadway Songs**	$14.95
00740249	**2. Jazz Standards**	$14.95
00740246	**3. Contemporary Hits**	$14.95
00740277	**4. '80s Gold**	$12.95
00740299	**5. Christmas Standards**	$15.95
00740281	**6. Disco Fever**	$12.95
00740279	**7. R&B Super Hits**	$12.95
00740309	**8. Wedding Gems**	$12.95
00740409	**9. Broadway Standards**	$14.95
00740348	**10. Andrew Lloyd Webber**	$14.95
00740344	**11. Disney's Best**	$14.99
00740378	**12. Ella Fitzgerald**	$14.95
00740350	**14. Musicals of Boublil & Schönberg**	$14.95
00740377	**15. Kelly Clarkson**	$14.95
00740342	**16. Disney Favorites**	$14.99
00740353	**17. Jazz Ballads**	$14.99
00740376	**18. Jazz Vocal Standards**	$16.99
00740375	**20. Hannah Montana**	$16.95
00740354	**21. Jazz Favorites**	$14.99
00740374	**22. Patsy Cline**	$14.95
00740369	**23. Grease**	$14.95
00740367	**25. ABBA**	$14.95
00740365	**26. Movie Songs**	$14.95
00740360	**28. High School Musical 1 & 2**	$14.95
00740363	**29. Torch Songs**	$14.95
00740379	**30. Hairspray**	$14.95
00740380	**31. Top Hits**	$14.95
00740384	**32. Hits of the '70s**	$14.95
00740388	**33. Billie Holiday**	$14.95
00740389	**34. The Sound of Music**	$15.99
00740390	**35. Contemporary Christian**	$14.95
00740392	**36. Wicked**	$15.99
00740393	**37. More Hannah Montana**	$14.95
00740394	**38. Miley Cyrus**	$14.95
00740396	**39. Christmas Hits**	$15.95
00740410	**40. Broadway Classics**	$14.95
00740415	**41. Broadway Favorites**	$14.99
00740416	**42. Great Standards You Can Sing**	$14.99
00740417	**43. Singable Standards**	$14.99
00740418	**44. Favorite Standards**	$14.99
00740419	**45. Sing Broadway**	$14.99
00740420	**46. More Standards**	$14.99
00740421	**47. Timeless Hits**	$14.99
00740422	**48. Easygoing R&B**	$14.99
00740424	**49. Taylor Swift**	$15.99
00740425	**50. From This Moment On**	$14.99
00740426	**51. Great Standards Collection**	$19.99
00740430	**52. Worship Favorites**	$14.99
00740434	**53. Lullabyes**	$14.99
00740438	**54. Lady Gaga**	$14.99
00740444	**55. Amy Winehouse**	$14.99
00740445	**56. Adele**	$14.99

MEN'S EDITIONS

00740248	**1. Broadway Songs**	$14.95
00740250	**2. Jazz Standards**	$14.95
00740251	**3. Contemporary Hits**	$14.99
00740278	**4. '80s Gold**	$12.95
00740298	**5. Christmas Standards**	$15.95
00740280	**6. R&B Super Hits**	$12.95
00740282	**7. Disco Fever**	$12.95
00740310	**8. Wedding Gems**	$12.95
00740411	**9. Broadway Greats**	$14.99
00740333	**10. Elvis Presley – Volume 1**	$14.95
00740349	**11. Andrew Lloyd Webber**	$14.95
00740345	**12. Disney's Best**	$14.95
00740347	**13. Frank Sinatra Classics**	$14.95
00740334	**14. Lennon & McCartney**	$14.99
00740335	**16. Elvis Presley – Volume 2**	$14.99
00740343	**17. Disney Favorites**	$14.99
00740351	**18. Musicals of Boublil & Schönberg**	$14.95
00740346	**20. Frank Sinatra Standards**	$14.95
00740358	**22. Great Standards**	$14.99
00740336	**23. Elvis Presley**	$14.99
00740341	**24. Duke Ellington**	$14.99
00740359	**26. Pop Standards**	$14.99
00740362	**27. Michael Bublé**	$14.95
00740364	**29. Torch Songs**	$14.95
00740366	**30. Movie Songs**	$14.95
00740368	**31. Hip Hop Hits**	$14.95
00740370	**32. Grease**	$14.95
00740371	**33. Josh Groban**	$14.95
00740373	**34. Billy Joel**	$14.99
00740381	**35. Hits of the '50s**	$14.95
00740382	**36. Hits of the '60s**	$14.95
00740383	**37. Hits of the '70s**	$14.95
00740385	**38. Motown**	$14.95
00740386	**39. Hank Williams**	$14.95
00740387	**40. Neil Diamond**	$14.95
00740391	**41. Contemporary Christian**	$14.95
00740397	**42. Christmas Hits**	$15.95
00740399	**43. Ray**	$14.95
00740400	**44. The Rat Pack Hits**	$14.99
00740401	**45. Songs in the Style of Nat "King" Cole**	$14.99
00740402	**46. At the Lounge**	$14.95
00740403	**47. The Big Band Singer**	$14.95
00740404	**48. Jazz Cabaret Songs**	$14.99
00740405	**49. Cabaret Songs**	$14.99
00740406	**50. Big Band Standards**	$14.99
00740412	**51. Broadway's Best**	$14.99
00740427	**52. Great Standards Collection**	$19.99
00740431	**53. Worship Favorites**	$14.99
00740435	**54. Barry Manilow**	$14.99
00740436	**55. Lionel Richie**	$14.99
00740439	**56. Michael Bublé – Crazy Love**	$14.99
00740441	**57. Johnny Cash**	$14.99
00740442	**58. Bruno Mars**	$14.99

MIXED EDITIONS

These editions feature songs for both male and female voices.

00740311	**1. Wedding Duets**	$12.95
00740398	**2. Enchanted**	$14.95
00740407	**3. Rent**	$14.95
00740408	**4. Broadway Favorites**	$14.99
00740413	**5. South Pacific**	$15.99
00740414	**6. High School Musical 3**	$14.99
00740429	**7. Christmas Carols**	$14.99
00740437	**8. Glee**	$15.99
00740440	**9. More Songs from Glee**	$19.99
00740443	**10. Even More Songs from Glee**	$15.99

FOR MORE INFORMATION, SEE YOUR LOCAL MUSIC DEALER,
OR WRITE TO:

HAL•LEONARD®
CORPORATION
7777 W. BLUEMOUND RD. P.O. BOX 13819 MILWAUKEE, WI 53213

Visit Hal Leonard online at
www.halleonard.com

Prices, contents, & availability subject to change without notice.

0811